In the City

Words by Eugene Booth
Pictures by Derek Collard

RAINTREE CHILDRENS BOOKS
Milwaukee • Toronto • Melbourne • London

Copyright © 1977, Macdonald-Raintree, Inc.

Library of Congress Number: 77-7949

   2 3 4 5 6 7 8 9 0 81 80 79 78

Printed and bound in the United States of America.

Library of Congress Cataloging in Publication Data

Booth, Eugene, 1940 —
    In the city.

    (A Raintree spotlight book)
    SUMMARY: Uses a city setting to stimulate such
activities as counting, noting visual differences,
and making up a story.
    [1.   City and town life]   I.   Collard, Derek.
II.   Title.
PZ7.B6467Ij   [E]   77-7949
ISBN 0-8393-0109-X lib. bdg.

In the City

Look at this busy city street.
How many cars and trucks do you see?
How many people?

Can you count the red things?
Can you count the round things?
What do you think will happen
to these people?

Look at what is going on.
Is it what you thought would happen?
How did you know?

Who is mad? Who is happy?
Who might be hurt?
Pretend you are a person in this picture.
What would you do?

1

2

3

4

Some of these cars are yellow.
Some of these cars are blue.
Some go left, some go right.
I can count them all. Can you?

How many cars are on the bridge?
How many cars are down below?
How many cars have stopped for gas?
How many cars are on the go?

Big and little, short and tall. Which car is largest? Which tree is small?

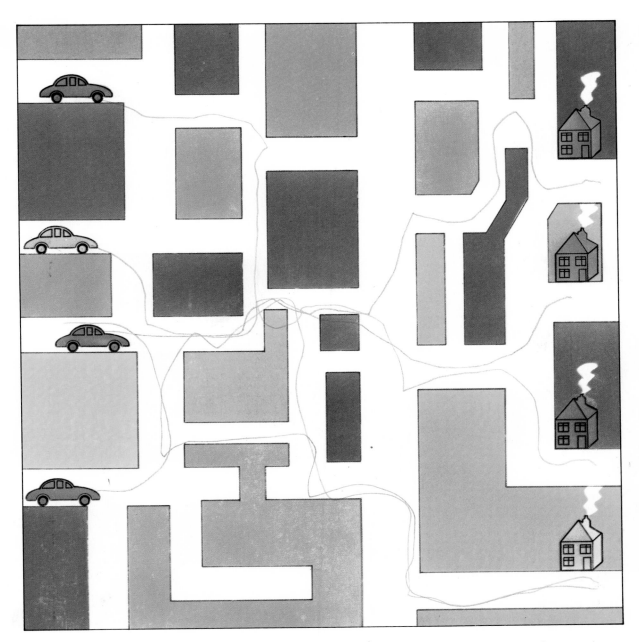

Each car on this page is the same color as a house. See if you can get each car home.

The city is a busy place.
What are all these people doing?

How many stores can you see?
What can you buy in each store?

13

Many people live in this house.
What is each person doing?

Can you do some of these things?
Which things do you like to do?
Tell a story about each person.

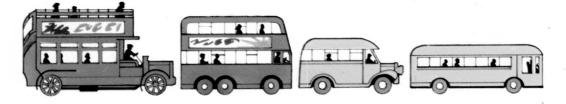

Count the big trucks, then the little
trucks. How many cars do you see?
Count the bikes for one person
and for two. How many buses are yellow?

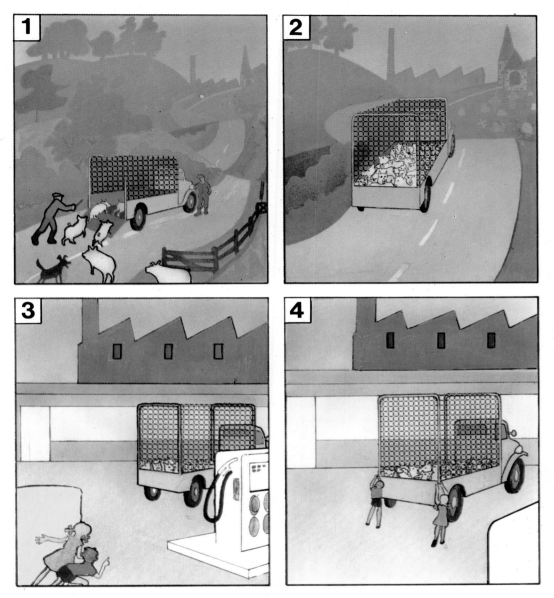

These four pictures tell a story.
What story do you think they tell?
How will the story end?

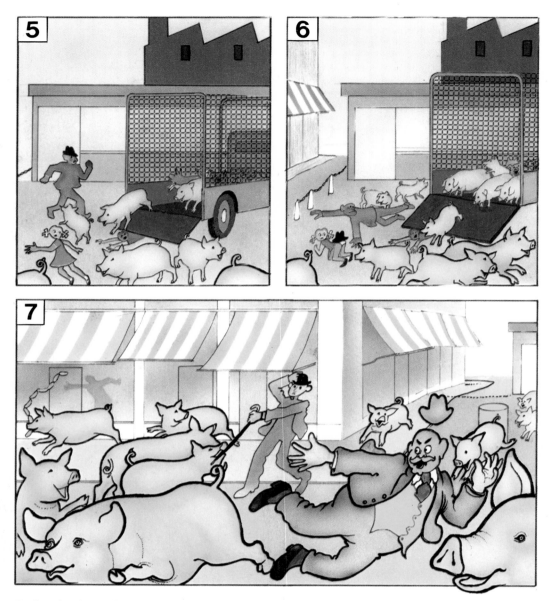

Finish the story by looking at the pictures. Was it the same story you made up?

What is wrong in this picture?
What else could go wrong?

Look at the shapes at the bottom of
the next page. Can you find them in
the picture?

What are the names of these shapes?